YOUR KNOWLEDGE HAS VALUE

Bibliographic information published by the German National Library:

The German National Library lists this publication in the National Bibliography; detailed bibliographic data are available on the Internet at http://dnb.dnb.de .

Imprint:

Copyright © 2016 GRIN Verlag, Open Publishing GmbH
Print and binding: Books on Demand GmbH, Norderstedt Germany
ISBN: 9783668283718

This book at GRIN:

http://www.grin.com/en/e-book/338528/lecture-notes-on-editorial-writing

Apuke Destiny Oberiri

Lecture Notes on Editorial Writing

GRIN Publishing

GRIN - Your knowledge has value

Since its foundation in 1998, GRIN has specialized in publishing academic texts by students, college teachers and other academics as e-book and printed book. The website www.grin.com is an ideal platform for presenting term papers, final papers, scientific essays, dissertations and specialist books.

Visit us on the internet:

http://www.grin.com/

http://www.facebook.com/grincom

http://www.twitter.com/grin_com

LECTURE NOTES ON EDITORIAL WRITING

DEPARTMENT OF MASS COMMUNICATION

TARABA STATE UNIVERSITY

COURSE OUTLINE

INTRODUCTION

It is quite acceptable that journalists and mass communicators primarily have the responsibility of informing, educating and entertaining members of the society. As an institution, the mass media could set agenda, preserve cultural heritage, as well as confer status on individuals or institutions in the society. To achieve these, however, different approaches, such as news reporting, features writing, news analysis, editorial writing and news commentaries, could be employed by journalists. This lecture explores editorial writing with particular emphasis on its meaning, history, characteristics and nature.

At the end of this unit, you should be able to:

• Define what an Editorial is

• Know the history of Editorials

• Explain the characteristics of Editorials

• Describe the nature of Editorials.

DEFINITION OF EDITORIAL

An editorial could be defined as a corporate voice of a media organisation on any given issue of public interest. Also known as the leader, the editorial is looked upon by Duyile (2005:63) as the "opinion of a newspaper simply written for the understanding of readers, leading them to take decisions on the issues being discussed." In a simple manner, the veteran journalist describes it as the explanatory text, the opinions of the newspaper on any topic. According to him, this could be an argument exhibiting the logical reasoning of a newspaper, using thoughts of the proprietor for the purpose of persuading the readers (audience) to either kick against or accept an idea, policy or an action based on facts available. Hoffman (2007:113) on the other hand, views an editorial as a "statement of opinion from an editor or publisher about you and your business or media coverage generated by news staff." In agreement with the above, Iyorkyaa (1996:4) define an editorial as "a journalistic essay which attempts to: a.

4

inform or explain; b. persuade or convince; c. stimulate insight in an entertaining or humorous manner." In their views, Okoro and Agbo (2003:125) capture the concept of the editorial as "a critical evaluation, interpretation and presentation of significant, contemporary events in such a way as to inform, educate, entertain and influence the reader." It could be inferred from the definitions above that an editorial is based on expression or corporate opinion which usually interprets issues from a deeper out-look and entertains the average reader with its substance and depth of analysis. Editorial writing has become a celebrated concept for serious-minded newspapers just as a news commentary is for broadcasting due to the opinion function of the mass media (Ate, 2006). However, an editorial is influenced by the newspaper policy and philosophy, ownership structure as well as political environment in which it operates.

Brief History of Editorials

What is today known as the editorial could be traced as far back in 1880 (Yaasa, 1996:6). This was the time in which the term Editorial was put to use as a label to mark clearly a statement of the editor's opinion. The term was used then to refer to an article written by the editor. However, in the 20th century, the coast of editorials became wide-spread. This was largely due to the fact that newspapers across the globe had made editorials to be occupying separate pages or spaces in their publications. Also around this period, certain newspapers the world over began placement of editorials on left hand pages, usually in front of the section. It is worthy to note that modern newspapers have significantly expanded and enriched the editorial page to the extent that it is been used to face lengthy opinions by columnists and guest writers. This trade mark is known as op-ed, meaning opposite the editorial page.

Features of an Editorial

An editorial topic or subject cannot emerge from the blue. (Ate, 2007). It usually comprises issues of topical interest that have been reported in the mass media by way of hard news or features, which attracts public attention and debate.

An editorial could, therefore, be said to have characteristics of news and features elements. More so, an editorial has other features like objectivity, precision, specialism and advocacy. These according to Ukonu (2005) are all incorporated into editorials for the fact that it is investigative, interpretative and newsy in nature. He contends that the editorial is a melting pot for all kinds of journalist writings.

An editorial also has some characteristics of a story because of its subjectivity biases. Editorials could be subjective in posture because their sources could emanate from thought-provoking letters to the editors which are often used for gauging public opinion on emerging controversial and topical issues of public interest.

An editorial is also characterized by borrowed ideas from other journalistic write-ups. This simply agrees with the fact that the editorial has some components of different journalistic write-ups.

Nature of Editorial

Editorial writing belongs to the print media genre. While other opinion pieces like articles, columns and essays are credited to individuals or joint writers, the editorial belongs to a newspaper as an institution – a social institution. (Ukonu, 2005).

Naturally, an editorial is more of a corporate view. It therefore carries an institutional flavour. This explains why terms like "we" or a newspaper's name is often used instead of "I" or the writer's name. Since it is an organisational affair, any credit or blame in an editorial usually goes to the organisation, rather than the individual.

SELF ASSESSMENT EXERCISE

1. In your own words, define Editorial.

2. Briefly trace the history of editorial and the changes in its trends from individual to corporate expression.

3. What are the features of an editorial?

4. Distinguish the nature of editorials from other forms of writing.

QUALITIES OF A GOOD EDITORIAL

INTRODUCTION

Editorial, just like human beings have qualities. This lecture shall discuss the qualities of editorial. This is aimed at assisting the student in writing a professionally acceptable editorial.

Qualities of a Good Editorial

It is important for a good editorial writer to imbibe certain guidelines on the concept of editorial writing. These guidelines will enable the writer to appreciate the qualities of a good editorial. Ate (2007), Onabajo (2000), Ukonu (2005), Okoro and Agbo (2003) capture the general hints guiding the concept of editorial writing. These are:

1. **Institutional Flavour** : The editorial must be written using the institutional name. It should be regarded as the corporate voice of the media establishment and not that of the individual.

2. **The Language should be plain and Unambiguous** : Whatever purpose is intended of an editorial, the writer should make the language simple, so it could be understood by the target audience. For the editorial writer to achieve this,

there is a need to avoid beating about the bush.

3. **Editorials should be exact and Straight-To-The-Point** : It is expected of a good editorial writer to make the point as it is. This is a good quality of editorial that makes it to be punchy and short.

4. It must be Human Interest Oriented: Man is generally interested in affairs of fellow men. He therefore looks for such knowledge. An editorial that has human interest is bound to win the affection of people, as they would get interested in it than others. It is therefore essential to make this a good quality of an editorial.

5. Editorials should be Catchy and Attention Arresting: A writer should avoid dull and weak editorials because they cannot create a desired effect on the target audience. Strong words that are persuasive in nature should be used in an editorial to make it catchy and attention-arresting.

6. It should be Original in Tone and Substance: Editorials are not copied from other newspapers. Rather, they are generated by ideas obtained from researches. Editorial writers should be original in the art and science of editorial writing. They should avoid copying other people's work, but rather contribute new ideas and agenda for public opinion.

7. It must be well Researched Just as it is mentioned above: Editorial writers should research before writing the editorial. This could make the editorial timely, authoritative and qualitative. A highly profound editorial is a product of good research.

8. Editorials should be Factual, Concrete and not speculative : Editorial writers should make sure that their opinion pieces are credible enough for publication. It is wise for such editorials to be cross-checked to avoid falsehood and ensure accuracy.

Capturing the qualities of a good editorial in harmony of the above views, Folarin (1998:36-38) identifies the general tips on editorial writing:

• select a current topic and stick to it, albeit looking at it from all relevant angles. Sometimes an advocacy or propagandistic editorial chooses a specific point of view and sticks to it, disregarding other possible angles. The purpose of the editorial decides the approach adopted

• find a sound premise for your position and let your reasoning on that premise be equally sound.

• make the editorial short and crisp. A long editorial is an aberration and must have a strong justification – such as a special occasion (military coup, an independence anniversary, the signing of a bilateral treaty etc). In many cases, long editorials are broken down into installments, each installment looking at a specific aspect of the topic. More than two editorials on a given topic becomes an "editorial campaign". Such campaigns are rare in Nigeria.

• the language of editorials, more than that of any other item in the paper, is expected to be flawless, since the editorial is the "intellectual powerhouse of the newspaper". The expression is forthright and masculine, and does not leave the reader in any doubt about the paper's position on the pertinent issue. Simplicity is not a leading quality of editorials in Nigeria. But each one should be clear, concise and definitive.

For any editorial to create the desired effect and win the affection of the audience, it must have the above qualities. It is therefore important for editorialists to have a mastery of what constitute good editorials. Good editorials are not supposed to be dull. They are not supposed to be emotional and illogical. They are not supposed to be based on rumour or untested facts but on concrete and logical facts. They are not supposed to be based on irrelevant issues but on topical issues of public interest. Good editorials must have a segmented audience but its message must be understood by all who are exposed to it. A good editorial must also have visual or pictorial qualities. As the reader is exposed to it, he or she should be able to appreciate the issue under probe in real terms.

SELF ASSESSMENT EXERCISE

Discuss the qualities of a good editorial.

PUBLIC OPINION AND EDITORIALS

Definitions of Public Opinion

Importance of Public Opinion

Formation of Public Opinion

Opinion Functions of Editorials

INTRODUCTION

The mass media are known for their roles in the formation of public opinion. Thus, this has earned them the title "the court of public opinion." This unit examines issues that revolve around the importance of public opinion and its formation. A thorough examination of the opinion function of editorials would be the focal point of discussion. This would enable the student to appreciate the importance of editorials in modern day newspapers.

At the end of this unit, you should be able to:

• define public opinion

• discuss the importance of public opinion

 • state the factors that are responsible for the formation of public opinion

• discuss the opinion function of editorials.

Definition of Public Opinion

Public opinion is, simply, the aggregate views of members of the society on a given significant issue, be it political, social or an economic one. Put simpler, public opinion is a collection of views and feelings of members of the public on current topical issues. Take for instance, the voting pattern of 2007 election. Public views can be harvested on the issue and the position of the public can be made known through the mass media.

Importance of Public Opinion

The mass media are indisputably the mouth piece of society. Because of the aggressive expansion of societies in recent times as a result of population explosion, the mass media remain the only sure voice or platform whereby members of society will express their feelings, views and opinions. Public opinion is useful or beneficial in the following ways:

i. **provides the resources for determining the current I mage of an individual or organization.** If, for instance, a political office holder wishes to measure or test his/her popularity, public opinion will be the way forward. The media will only take the individual concern to the court of public opinion and either the vote of confidence or no confidence would be passed on the person. The same thing could be applicable to an organization that wishes to measure its profile in the eyes of the public.

ii. **Reveals need for social change.** Social change, according to Wilmot (1985:174) cited in Ojo (2004), is the alteration in the sources or organization of society or its component parts overtime. Mac Gee et al (1977:589) cited in Ojo (op cit) describes social change as the transformation in patterns of social organization or activity. An adage says nothing is permanent except change. The mass communicator through his interaction with diverse members of the society is an agent of change. The mass communicator keeps a tab on human and organization behaviours and in line with public position or opinion may champion the cause of social change in a society.

iii. **Predicts financial and developmental future of an organization.** The mass media may keep its watchful eyes on a particular organization and predict the organization's future financial status through the help of public opinion.

iv. **Provides raw materials for research purposes**. By exposing some grey areas of a phenomenon through public opinion or debate, researchers could benefit much in the art and science of public opinion.

v. Aids policy formulation and planning in society. Through public opinion, government can know the views of the people and can formulate policies for their good governance.

Formation of Public Opinion

Generally, controversial issues are batteries for formation of public opinion. However, public opinion can be formed in other diverse ways. These include:

• Through the mass media. That is the expression of people's views through Radio, TV, Newspapers, and Magazines.

• Peer groups. A group of people moving together and sharing common ties and influences.

• Pressure group and political parties. Pressure group, professional leanings and political parties provide a bazaar of information that forms and shapes public opinion.

• Symposia and lectures. Symposia and public lectures provide avenues for brainstorming of ideas whose molecules can be used in constructing public opinion.

• Election – Political advertisements and other kinds of electioneering campaigns often provoke important public issues that result in formation of public opinion.

• Individual orientation or background. A person who, by geographical, professional or social background, is thoroughly exposed to public issues or debates can serve as a useful resource in the formation of public opinion

Opinion Functions of Editorials

There is a striking relationship between public opinion and editorial writing. Issues in the mass media, you will agree, may start at the running-fever level (insignificant level) but later explode into public knowledge. It is at this stage that the editorial writer comes in either to support or oppose the vexed issue in the court of public opinion. Editorials in modern newspapers and magazines, according to Ate (2007:21-28), perform the following functions:

i. Criticise or attack socio-political, economic and moral dilemmas of the society. An editorialist sometimes performs the job of a human rights activist raising alarm on blatant abuse or annihilation of certain norms and acceptable social order in the society. Exploitative and autocratic government policies can be attacked by editorials. On the side of the governed, when a particular section of the society decides, for instance, to take laws into its hand, editorials are bound to criticize such an anomaly.

ii. Illuminate the day's intelligence. By throwing more light to complex issues of the day, editorials often try to look at the two sides of an issue. They highlight and analyse the strengths and weaknesses of public issues while proffering solutions to complex issues of public concern.

iii. Bring to fore debatable issues and provide an intellectual compass for society to discuss and resolve burning issues. Editorials give direction for discussion and resolution of burning issues in the society. They provoke debate on diverse issues of public concern especially for the elites. iv. Defend the underdogs in the society. In every given society, there exist different dimensions of natural and artificial economic gaps between the rich and the poor, the powerful and the powerless, the educated and the uneducated, etc. When the rich, for instance, tend to unjustifiably exploit and manipulate the poor, editorials rise up in defense of the latter. The relationship among different members of the society is often monitored by the media and an advocacy role played by editorials to defend the course of the wretched of the earth.

v. To influence policy formulation or decision making on certain issues. Editorials galvanise policy makers to set proactive agenda for good governance of the society.

Capturing the characteristics of editorials in harmony with the aforementioned functions, Idemili, cited in Uwakwe (2005:107-108), observes:

a. That the editorial helps the reader to bring order out of chaos of news.

b. That on the editorial page, special reporters or columnists have a place, for explaining behind-the-scene events and that freedom of style and deep backgrounding is permitted. c. That the editorial can fight battles for the newspaper reader.

d. That the editorial plays agenda-setting functions or role; exposes public debate, the good and bad ideas in circulation.

e. That the editorial page should give readers the opportunity to air their views by providing space for letters to the editor. f. That the editorial makes room for the editor to express his views.

g. That the editorial serves as a source of personality to the newspaper.

vii. Appeal or Persuade. Editorials appeal to or persuade the readers to accept the rightness or wrongness of an issue. Some editorials often woo individual members of the society, corporate bodies or government to accept a particular course of action for the interest of the society. Such editorials are sandwiched with concrete facts and spice-up with tantalizing persuasive techniques which create indelible marks on the psyche of readers.

A good and powerful editorial usually has impact. In Nigeria, for instance, good editorials often galvanise policy formulation on the side of government and relevant stakeholders for the betterment of the society. On the side of the governed, editorials mobilize them either to reject or accept a policy or a burning issue of the day.

Editorials can in a detailed manner, indicate, inform and entertain members of the public and divergent issues in the society. Ideas harvested from editorials can also help in preserving the nation's sacred institutions like marriage, religion, etc. Through broadcast commentaries, members of the community can be mobilized to participate in meaningful developmental projects in the society. Such projects may include head count, election, immunization exercise, to mention only a few. Editorials can create a pathway for legislators for instance, to initiate bills that would eventually become laws in the nation's statute books. If an editorial is to create impact on its audience, it must reflect the wisdom, integrity and voice of the society.

An impact-creating editorial must represent the hopes and aspirations of the community in which the newspaper is located or published.

SELF ASSESSMENT EXERCISE

Define public opinion. 2. Outline the importance of public opinion. 3. Identify at least six factors that can be used in the formation of public opinion. 4. Discuss the functions of editorials in the mass media.

EDITORIALS AND OTHER FORMS OF WRITING

INTRODUCTION

Editorials and other forms of newspaper write-ups are based on subjective opinion about issues. This is unlike straight forward news reporting which is mostly objective and based on facts. This unit examines the relationship between editorials and other forms of writing, such as features, columns and news.

By the end of this unit, you should be able to: • discuss the relationship between editorials and factual news reporting • appreciate the relationship between editorials and features • state the relationship between editorials and columns.

Editorial and News

For a rewind, the editorial is the corporate expression of media organisation on given issues of public interest, while news is the recounting of factual and timely events in the society. It is instructive to know that editorials are "opinionated" or subjective, while news is objective in nature. Editorials are written out of news stories, while news is influenced by events, reports and the audience. The major elements of news are: • Timeliness • Proximity • Oddities • Prominence • Consequences • Human interest.

Straightforward news reporting or factual news is a kind of report that says it as it is. Factual news serves as sources for editorials and features, as most issues addressed in editorials do emanate from news reports. Editorials also stimulate news. This is clearly shown when the public reacts to editorial contents either in support or objection of an issue. It is, therefore, clear that both concepts complement each other.

Editorial and Features

Editorial writing is research oriented. The same thing is applicable to features writing. A feature is a creative journalistic article which informs, explains, analyses, interprets, and exposes issues for the sake of readers. Awoyinfa and Igwe (1991:5) describe a feature as a "colourful story about people, events, places, life… It is written in an interesting and creative manner with information drawn from people involved, eyewitnesses, experts on the subjects and those affected by the subjects". Both features and editorials give room for deeper and logical analysis of issues. However, Okoro and Agbo (2003:96) provide the parting point between features and editorials as follows: (a) Most features carry bylines, i.e they are signed by their writers. Usually, editorials do not carry bylines. (b) Features can be accompanied by illustrations. In most cases, editorials are not illustrated (photographic illustrations). (c) Features are usually the result of individual effort, while editorials are the result of group effort, that is, the editorial board.

Editorials and Columns

An editorial is a journalistic article or essay which critically and rationally informs, educates and entertains its target audience on sociopolitical and economic issues of the day. A column on the other hand is an article which carries the personality, style, and individual identity of the writer. The Longman Dictionary of Contemporary English defines a column as an article on a particular subject or by a particular writer that appears regularly in a newspaper or a magazine. Editorials and columns have striking resemblance in tone and substance, especially public affairs columns. That notwithstanding, columns and editorials have some demarcation lines. According to Onabajo (2000), most editorials have institutional flavours while columns have personal flavours, a distinction that goes beyond the use of "we" and "I". In writing an editorial, the word "we" or the name of the newspaper or magazine is often used as an attestation of the corporate concern while "I" is used in columns to showcase personal appeal. In columns, the author's byline and style are made manifest in the writeup. This is opposed to editorial writing where all credits, glories and blames, as the case may be, go to the media establishment and not to an individual. Duyile (2005:69) gives the demarcation line between columns and editorials. According to him, "writing a column is not writing an editorial. It is a kind of feature which expresses your personality to readers. The readers will always remember you for your expressions, your style, and your treatment of issues from your own personal ways." Under columns, the writer's names or pseudonym can be used but this is not applicable to editorial writing.

SELF ASSESSMENT EXERCISE

Explain the relationship between editorial and factual news reporting.

2. Describe the meeting and parting points of features and editorials.

3. Explain the differences between editorials and columns.

TYPES OF EDITORIALS

There are three basic types of editorials. These are: i. Interpretative Editorials ii. Controversial Editorials iii. Explanatory Editorials

Interpretative Editorial: These are written to explain issues at stake. They, therefore, place factual points for readers to assess and decide a right action to take. They could be positive, negative or even neutral to issues, depending on the views of the media organisation.

Let's take a look at a sample of this kind of editorial.

Nigeria's Future

A report by a US intelligence agency on the future of Nigeria by 2020 has generated concerns. The global report of the US National Intelligence Council examined the social, political and economic future of countries and continents, identified areas of strengths and weaknesses worth consolidating or redressing, and made some projections.

Specifically, the report predicted that Nigeria might break up within 15 years if the leaders disregard people's wish and insist on an unworkable union. According to the report, the country's "leaders are locked up in a bad marriage that all dislike but dare not leave." The document expresses the possibility of "a junior officer coup that could destabilize the country to the extent that open warfare breaks out in many parts in a sustained manner;" adding rightly that a failed Nigeria will be difficult to reconstitute.

The report also notes that Africa's hope of benefitting from globalization will depend on the extent to which each country improves governance, reins in corruption, resolves conflicts, and firms up the rule of law. Leadership, the report says, will be the key to progress for sub-Saharan countries that are lucky to evolve it. The report does not spare the US, which it says might lose its global economic dominance to upcoming China and India.

While dismissing the report as "glib talk" by detractors, President Mohammadu Buhari has confessed that the gloomy forecast poses a serious challenge to him and all Nigerians. He has, therefore, passed the report to the National Assembly for action.

There is no doubt that almost everyone wants a united Nigeria. But the injustices that precipitated the 30-month civil war in 1967 appear to have grown deeper and more widespread. Over the years, successive governments have failed to forge a national identity. So, the citizens still feel more comfortable sticking to their ethnic identities. Since democracy reemerged in 1999, hundreds of thousands of people have been killed in ethno-religious crises that sprouted from the unsettled national question over indigene/settler dichotomy. There are standing ethnic militias in the north, south, east and west. Just recently, President Obasanjo reportedly gave out several millions of naira as ransom to stave off the threat to blow up oil installations by a Niger Delta militia group.

Except the deceitful ones, therefore, only a few would require a US intelligence to predict that Nigeria's fragile unity may snap if urgent steps are not taken to redress a flawed and unjust structure that has only fueled mass poverty and frustration. For now, the ruling class may continue to delude itself that there are no dangers ahead. Blinded by the filthy reward they get from a corrupt and dysfunctional system, the nation's unruly politicians often wrongly assume that citizens will forever tolerate injustice via rigged elections; executive rascality in flagrantly disobeying Supreme Court verdicts; and abuse of incumbency powers to brutalize or kill political opponents.

Buhari's anger that government's ongoing promising reforms were not reckoned with in foreseeing a brighter future for Nigeria is instructive. But the truth is that the reforms are half-hearted and so yield slow, insignificant and unnoticeable returns. Six years of reforms, for instance, has produced a more epileptic regime of power supply, posing a serious threat to industrialization and job creation. That is just one indication that the nation's economy is far from being export-oriented and, therefore, vulnerable to the adverse impacts of globalization.

To prevent the doomsday forecast from being fulfilled, the nation's leaders must be bold enough to dismantle an unjust fiscal structure that has alienated the constituent parts. The nation's unity depends on how quickly the centre is whittled down for a truly federal Nigerian state to emerge.

Controversial Editorials:

Controversial editorials are written with the particular mission or mandate to propagate a particular or specific point of view. Such editorials often attempt to convince the reader on the desirability or inevitability of a particular issue while painting the opposing side in bad light. These kinds of editorials are either positive or negative. There is no room for neutrality in such editorials because they can out rightly support or oppose an issue with all vehemence (Ate 2007:16). Below is a specimen of a controversial editorial.

Kalu's Comedy of Errors

The People's Democratic Party (PDP) is undoubtedly a big party. Its bigness derives from a lot of variables. These variables include size, geographical spread, religious spread, membership and even quality of individual members. For a country whose previous democratic collapse could be partly traced to the failure of electoral politics, the PDP held hope for the sustenance of democracy in Nigeria.

Yet, its strength contains the ingredients of its weakness. As a rainbow coalition, it was an amalgam of all-comers. There was no attempt to use the factor of antecedents to sift membership. The resultant effect is the emergence of some leaders who ordinarily should not be admitted into a serious party. More embarrassing and depressing is the fact that some of them hold offices that can make one equate them with the party.

Such a person is Governor Orji Uzor Kalu of Abia State. Right from the beginning, he comes across as an undisciplined party-man. He seems to have an inflated opinion, not only of his popularity in his state of Abia, but of an erroneous position in Nigerian history. He plays all forms of pranks to reconfirm his fable of historical expectation. He situates his ambition on very faulty premises and dishes out to himself over-seasoned salad of political relevance. Ordinarily, one should not be bothered about such illusion except for the Yoruba adage which counsels that if your neighbour chooses to eat dangerous insects and you refuse to caution him, his restlessness at the dead of the night would disturb your own sleep.

Governor Kalu's latest antics relate to an alleged assassination threat on his life by Chief Tony Anenih, the Chairman Board of Trustees of the ruling PDP. An accusation of murder or threat of it is so grievous that the ingredients of such accusation must be unassailable. In Kalu's case, he said his Deputy Governor, relayed to him the threat of assassination after

20

meeting casually with Chief Anenih. The Deputy Governor has since denied that he relayed such a message. In fact, his memo to Governor Kalu on the chance meeting with Anenih does not contain such an accusation.

But Kalu's bag of mischief and character assassination seems inexhaustible. He had earlier accused the same Anenih of collecting over N300 billion Naira as minister without anything to show for it. Official figures revealed that within the period of his ministerial responsibility, Anenih collected a little over N200 billion. One would ordinarily expect a state governor to speak with reliable facts and figures in honour of the respect of the office he holds. Even on the assassination threat, Kalu added a cheap shot to seek the support of the Yoruba people by alleging that Anenih said he would deal with him, the way he dealt with the late Chief Bola Ige. It does not stand to sense within a short chance meeting to be so frivolous and flippant like a chatter-box to let so loose. More so, when the meeting was in the presence of other people.

A simple dictum in law is that, he who asserts must prove. The onus of proof lies on Kalu. But it seems to us that he has not, and cannot, discharge such a burden of proof. The problem is compounded by the juvenile reliance on his mother anytime he chooses to run into problems. When he engaged in an undue adversary relationship with President Obasanjo sometime ago, it was his mother who was raising the olive branch for peace. In the current one, the flag of surrender is being raised by his mother. Governor Kalu, as a public office holder, must be told to grow or at worst, be made to grow. The image of a baby who causes problems outside and runs to mama at home is repulsive at this stage of our political development.

The Hope believes that Governor Kalu's dangerous drama can heat up the polity and even perhaps, dislocate it. The PDP as a political party should by now have an effective machinery of disciplining its members irrespective of how highly placed. The PDP for now holds in its hands the destiny of this country and the action or inaction of any of its members can truncate the democratic experiment. This is why it must urgently cage Kalu and polish him to measure up to the image of a matured state governor.

Explanatory Editorials:

These usually present a catalogue of issues at the doorstep of readers for their judgment or appraisal. Here, a writer only opens-up thought-provoking issues for readers' attention, by identifying and explaining it and allowing the reader to proffer solutions. Here is a sample of an explanatory editorial. Taylor and the Interpol

Since the United Nations-backed Special Court for the trial of those who bear the greatest responsibility for the war crimes in Sierra Leone indicted and issued a warrant of arrest on Charles Taylor of Liberia, several curious twists have dogged the development. The indictment and the warrant of arrest were made on Taylor in June, last year, while he was still a sitting Liberian president attending peace talks in Ghana on his country's civil war. His status as a sitting president presented a dilemma for his arrest, for it would contradict the law of nations to arrest an incumbent president. Of course, Nigeria, Ghana and other African leaders in attendance at that meeting rightfully ignored the order and never arrested Taylor.

Subsequently, owing to the pressure for peace in Liberia, Nigeria, reportedly backed by the United States' government, offered asylum to Taylor in order to remove him from the Liberian political scene and create some prospects for peace. During his tour of four African countries in July, last year, President George W. Bush was reported to have said that Nigeria's offer of asylum to Taylor was timely and the best solution to the Liberian conflict.

In fact, the peace that is gradually returning to that country today is partly a function of the removal of Taylor from Liberia via his asylum in Nigeria. But the curious twist and irony to it all is that the same United States government implicitly flawed the asylum by offering a $2 million ransom on Taylor. Although the ransom on Taylor has been fruitlessly denied by the US government, the International Police, Interpol, has followed the US' footsteps to issue a warrant of arrest on Taylor. And since Interpol's own warrant of arrest, a British firm has offered to kidnap Taylor in Nigeria.

Without prejudice to the merit of the Special Court's case against Taylor, what we caution here is against using it to trample on Nigeria's independence, sovereignty and territorial integrity. By putting a ransom on Taylor, and by subsequent warrant of arrest by the Interpol, an encouragement is being given to international brigands to violate Nigeria's sovereignty by illegally abducting Taylor against the will of the Nigerian government. Although Taylor has become a sufficient albatross to the Nigerian government, great care should be taken to ensure that he is not forcibly removed or abducted from Nigeria by any gang, whether sponsored by a foreign government, organization or not. Meanwhile, the Nigerian government should seriously spare a thought on how to dispose off the Taylor matter in order to bring these undue wrangling and harassment of Nigeria to an end.

It is instructive to state that some communication experts consider types of editorials from the perspective of the functions they perform. Uwakwe (2005: 111-112) captures the following types of editorial:

1. **Persuasive Editorial**: This type attempts to influence the reader to a cause. It tries to convince. It is frequently found in the dailies. To be able to present a good persuasive editorial, the writer has to "play up" the two sides to the coin. This will show that even though the writer has taken side, he is not out of prejudice because he has been deemed to have carefully weighted all the issues before taking a stand.

2. **Praise Editorial:** Editors cannot sometimes help but pay compliments for achievements. Such achievements could be individual or corporate.

3. **Explanatory Editorial:** This is also called the Expository Editorial. The purpose is to provide answers to questions lurking in the minds of readers. This, the editor can achieve through furnishing the reader with adequate information. This kind of editorial thrives on some sorts of interpretation.

4. Attack Editorial: This type of editorial berates an individual, public figure or corporate organisation for irresponsible behaviour. This kind of editorial protects the "watchdog" role of the press.

5. Crusading Editorial: Some events demand that a news organ fight for a particular cause. This is especially if the issue in question has generated some controversies and divided opinions. Editorials in support of such issues are known to be crusading in nature.

TUTOR-MARKED ASSIGNMENT List and explain the different types of editorial you know.

SOURCING THE EDITORIAL MATERIALS

Editorial materials can be sourced primarily from topical events that are reported from the mass media. The reported events must be captivating and of public interest (Ate, 2006). Other sources are as follows:

• **Internet**: Editorial writers in a computer-minded society can browse through the net and download relevant materials to write or enrich an editorial.

• **Public and Printed Records**: It is important to note that catalogues of records exist, documenting society's doings and misdoings. The editorial or leader writer can reach out to such records, e.g taxes, marriages, books, journals, government gazettes, biographies, Assembly proceedings Constitutions, etc. Little wonder, an anonymous reporter in Botch and Muller (1978:78) justified the importance of printed records thus: "Do anything from records that you can, because the records will stand and they will be there when people run out on you".

• **Social Functions**: A good editorial writer is not supposed to be a social illiterate. He/she must be rich in human relations and mix freely with people of different classes in order to get insight into the goings in the society. Attending parties, conferences, seminars, etc with the top shots in the society would help the editorial writer to understand their likes and dislikes and that would assist the editorialist in making profound analysis concerning the people in question.

• **Law Enforcement Officers**: An editorial writer can get additional information on his subject matter from the law enforcement officers like policemen, state security service men, etc if the issue under probe demands their attention.

• **Experts**: Professional and highly technical issues would compel the editorial writer to contact the appropriate experts. For instance, it will be necessary for an editorial writer to clear a controversial legal issue from a lawyer before writing. That would prevent the editorial writer from committing a costly mistake. Medical doctors, engineers, educationalists, etc can also be contacted for scoops in their own disciplines by the editorial writer.

• **Files**: Here, you have things like press clips which are usually classified according to subject matter for bibliographical exactitude. The editorial writer can also keep files of important events and related materials carefully dated and arranged for easy referencing.

• Libraries: Books of all kind, thesauruses, dictionaries, encyclopedias, almanacs, maps and charts etc can be obtained from the library for use in the course of writing an editorial.

• Specialized Sources: E.g Embassies, Nigerian Office of Statistics, INEC, Population Bureau, etc.

Review Questions: As an editorial writer, list the sources you can use in obtaining your data?.

QUALITIES OF GOOD EDITORIAL WRITERS

INTRODUCTION

Writing an editorial is usually a challenging task which involves team work. It is a collective efforts made by editorial board members. Editorials are assumed to be the back-bone of serious minded newspaper houses. Editorial writers are expected to acquire certain skills and qualities for effective discharge of their responsibilities. Being a corporate voice of newspapers, an editorial should be written by experienced and tested professionals and not just any body. This unit examines the ingredients of a good editorial writer.

Qualities of Good Editorial Writer

Never, can editorial writing be looked upon as a simple form of journalistic writing, that can be carried out by anybody. Professionally, it is tasking and demands good skills and qualities by whosoever aspires to be a writer. In order to live above water level, Ate (2007:8-10) identifies certain qualities that a good editorial writer should possess. These are:

a) Intellectual curiosity: This refers to ability to probe issues from academic and critical point of view.

b) Analytical mind: The editorial writer must be able to look deep at the pros and cons of an issue and harmonize both the opposing and supportive variables in an editorial superstructure.

c) Mastery of language: An editorialist must have a good command of the language in which the editorial is to be written. For an English speaking audience, for instance, a good command of English language is a non-negotiating factor. It is, indeed, a child of necessity.

d) Care for details: In editorial writing, issues are supposed to be logically and meticulously thrashed. It is only people who care for details that can unveil tiny but significant molecules underlying any conceptual phenomenon under probe.

e) Good knowledge and professional skills of writing for the mass media: The fact that somebody is a professor or doctorate degree holder in an area does not automatically make him/her a good editorial writer. In fact, there are some academics that can make a monumental mockery of editorial writing if they are not drilled in the art of writing for the mass media. An editorial writer needs to understand the workings of mass media outfits including the house style of the establishment he/she is writing for. The knowledge of writing for the mass media is very crucial for any editorial writer.

f) Rational Reasoning: Editorial Writing is a serious-minded business for serious-minded people. It is a house that cannot be built on bricks of emotionalism which cannot stand erect in the sea of reasoning. Strong and profound editorials can only be built on rational and logical raw materials mixed with concrete facts.

g) Knack for research: Editorial writing is research-oriented and therefore an editorial writer must love the art and science of research. He/she must be a curious and searching being with good leg work.

h) Nose for news: Since most editorials emerged from the controversies surrounding some news stories, it is expedient for an editorial writer to have nose for news. The understanding of what constitute "good" news by an editorial writer would in no small measure add a cubit in the analysis and interpretation of news in form of an editorial.

SELF ASSESSMENT EXERCISE 1. Discuss the basic functions of editorial board members. 2. John Kuhe is an aspiring editorial writer. Educate him on the qualities of a good editorial writer.

THE STRUCTURE OF AN EDITORIAL

A typical editorial has four parts. These are: Title, Introduction, Body and Conclusion. 1. **The Editorial Title:** This defines or introduces the editorial. It should be active, arresting and less wordy. Because titles serve as windows to editorials, they should not be dull, ambiguous or misleading. Rather, they should be sharp, punchy and catchy. For composing a good editorial title, Anim (1996:94) provided some useful hints.

• Some of the best titles are questions. e.g - Can NEPA improve?

• The who, what, why and how are useful in editorial heads. E.g - Who shot Ibru? - What a country! - Who runs the economy: Central Bank or IMF? - How to stop the touts?

• Sometimes looking at common sayings, short quotes and adages may lead to a good title. For example, "Arise O Compatriots" from the National Anthem can form the title of an editorial calling for national solidarity. - "Who can bell the cat"? This adage can be the title of an attack editorial on vacillation.

2. The Lead or "Intro": Next to the title is the lead which is simply the first paragraph of the leader or editorial. Like the editorial title, the lead or introduction must be captivating and juicy in order to compel the reader to read the entire editorial. A good leader must be able to sustain the interest earlier aroused by a tantalizing title. Depending on the creative prowess and experience of the editorial writer, any kind of lead, be it question lead, contrast lead, freak lead, direct address lead, etc would perform the magic, if is well crafted. On a general note, the introduction according to Anim (1996:95) contains:

(1) the news peg (2) the focus of the editorial (3) explores the tone presaged in the title Sample of an editorial intro in an editorial titled

"Nigerian Universities and world ranking"

The latest worldwide universities' ranking shows that Nigerian universities have dropped out of reckoning because of the poor quality and scope of research conducted by indigenous academics. No Nigerian university featured on the world best 500 universities list. Indeed from the African continent, only University of Cape Town, South Africa made the list. More embarrassing was the fact that even among contending universities in Africa, the best Nigerian university was ranked number 44, trading behind some universities in Kenya, South Africa and Ghana. (Source: The Guardian, May 25, 2007, page 14)

3. The Body: This contains the meat and substance of the editorial. It is the place where the props and cons of an issue are analyzed; conflicts of different colours are raised and resolved in the body of an editorial. The body of the editorial provides a platform for editorial reaction. Editorial reaction concerns itself with the stand or position of a newspaper on an issue. A good editorial body must be coherent and logical in presentation and analyses of data. There must be page unity and harmony of words and ideas in the body of the editorial. In a persuasive editorial, Anim (1996:99) observes that this section contains "the argument – evidence of fairness, credibility, appeal to emotions, if need be, and knowledgeability, comparisms, contrasts, statistics are contained in this section". Sample of the body of editorial from an editorial – "Nigerian Universities and world ranking" earlier cited.

The Nigerian academic is not lucky. He is entitled to attend international conferences about once in two years. If he must attend other conferences, he is required to look for funding from other sources. Reputable journals which were published in the universities of Ibadan, Lagos, Nsukka and Ife in the past have all disappeared due to poor funding. For example, the University of Ibadan used to be a reference point to international scholars of African history and culture. Those were the halcyon days of professors Kenneth Dike, Festus Ade Ajayi and Tekena Tamuno, etc. Indeed, Nigerian universities hosted academics and students from all regions of the world. These days, only refugees come to Nigerian universities to study. While others universities are expanding their library facilities, some federal universities have closed down departmental libraries. Ironically, most of our libraries are stocked with old volumes, with cramped-up spaces for the teeming population of students. Yale University has over one hundred libraries. Harvard makes about $25bn from endowments alone. With these funds, scholars have no problem whatsoever embarking on research and publishing their findings. The Nigerian government ought to take education more seriously, (Source: The Guardian, May 25, 2007).

4. **Conclusion**: Conclusion is the last part of an editorial. Usually, conclusion may be a re-affirmation of earlier position or idea advocated by the editorial writer in the body of the editorial. It may serve as an amplifier of a strong and potent view earlier put across in the course of writing. In handling the conclusion of an editorial, dangling modifiers and redundant words must be avoided.

TUTOR-MARKED ASSIGNMENT A good editorial writer must appreciate the importance of all segments of an editorial. Discuss.

GUIDES FOR GOOD EDITORIAL WRITING

Editorial writing is tasking and needs proactive planning and creativity to accomplish its mission. The major ingredients for determining editorial subjects are the policy and philosophy of the newspaper organization. Duyile (2005:64) however provides certain guides for good editorial writing. These are: 1) Get all your facts at your finger tips before making an outline of the editorial. 2) Be exhaustive in your fact finding for purposes of objectivity. 3) Let there be consistency in your paper's editorial opinions. 4) Be upright in your views and aggressive in your expression to drive your point home. 5) A good and respectable newspaper is not obscene-in its use of language in its editorials... Dignity in editorial is an indispensable factor in this respect. The more dignified the editorial, the more respect a newspaper receives from the society.

In what he considered as tips on editorial writing, Folarin (1998:36) xrayed the following:

• Select a current topic and stick to it, albeit looking at it from all relevant angles. • Find a sound premise for your position and let your reasoning based on that premise be equally sound.

• Make the editorial short and crisp. A long editorial is an aberration and must have a strong justification – such as a special occasion (a military coup, an independence anniversary, a signing of a bilateral treaty, etc)

• The language of editorials, more than that of any other item in the paper, is expected to be flawless, since the editorial is the "intellectual powerhouse of the newspaper."

Determinants of Editorial Subjects

Many factors may be considered in determining a subject for editorials. However, some major ones as considered by Ate (2007:48-50) are as follows:

1. Ensure that the topic is relevant and timely

2. The topic chosen might be local but the treatment should not be parochial

3. Editorial topic should be drawn from socio-political and economic issues

4. Topics could be borne out of the desire to amaze or amuse.

Ensure that the Topic is Relevant and Timely: In order to achieve this, the editorialist must factor into consideration the way and manner people converse with one another. In every society, people converse basically in three ways – (a) people talk about people (b) people talk about things/events (c) people talk ideas. Editorials that focus on people discussing people are likely going to be pedestrian in approach and may invoke the temptation of using foul or abusive language. Such editorials are hardly profound as they provide avenues for character assassination rather than opportunities for robust societal thinking. Editorials that deal with people discussing things or events are a little bit advanced and more acceptable than the first – people talking about people. However, these editorials cannot stand erect in the market place of ideas because they lack the fundamental oxygen that shapes public opinion or enliven public discourse. The best kinds of editorial are those whose platforms are erected on ideas. Ideas are vehicles that drive or move the society forward. Therefore, ideas oriented or anointed editorials are the most profound and celebrated ones.

• **Topic Might be Local but the Treatment should not be Parochial**: In writing an editorial master piece, a local, conservative and unusual topic could be raised but its treatment should be sound and logical. The writer should be able to bring out issues from the local event that are of national or international significance.

• **Editorial Topics should be Drawn from Socio-Political and Economic Issues**: The above would enable the editorialist to juxtapose thorough background of the event with clear illumination of the day's intelligence for the enrichment of public opinion, forecast the probable outcome of some issues and pass a moral judgment on same.

• **Topics could be Borne out of the Desire to Amaze or Amuse**: There is no gainsaying the fact editorial writing is a serious-minded affair. However, it is not all the times that the writer would feed the audience with serious-minded stuff. There are some situations where an editorial topic could be given light treatment to entertain the audience while feeding them with concrete facts. This is done to ease their tension and dilute the stress that usually goes with analysis of burning issues.

SELF ASSESSMENT EXERCISE 1. State the guides to good editorial writing.

2. Enumerate factors for determining editorial subjects

HOW TO WRITE EDITORIALS (PRACTICAL)

Editorial writing is a task that requires diligence and creativity by a writer. It is not enough for one to source for materials and arrive at a good editorial. A writer must be sound and logical in presenting the data. The editorial topic should be current, meaningful and in-depth in all ramifications. The editorial should reflect the socio-political and economic values of the society. There is a great need for the writer to be disciplined in selection of words. Such a writer should never loose focus of the ideas he/she is putting across in an editorial. The language of the editorial should be simple but mature in style in order to show seriousness. Every writer of editorial must/should endeavour to recognize the philosophy and editorial policy of his newspaper house, while taking a position on an issue of public interest. Ossai (2002) cited by Aneato and Onabajo (2007:64-65) identifies six stages in writing an editorial.

• The first stage is conducting research or the fact-finding stage.

An editorial written in a hurry without proper research could be shallow and woolly.

• The brainstorming exercise of an editorial conference is another stage.

• This is followed by outlining of points to be used in the writing.

• The next stage is forming opinion on the issue.

• Give another check on your materials to ensure accuracy.

• Finally, give a brief background, which should be concise and then say what you want to accomplish intelligently and withdraw.

THE EDITORIAL AUDIENCE

All forms of writing generally have audiences. So, it is with editorials. There are three categories of editorial audience. These are, the very skeptical audience, the very selective audience, and the obscure or obstinate audience. A good knowledge of editorial audience is important because it enables a writer to package his message to the right readers with excellent impact.

Ate (2007:41-42) examined these audiences in details.

The Very Skeptical Audience: These are sophisticated audiences with high aura of excellence. They question facts, figures, grammar, tone, style and content of every editorial until they are satisfied. They are the learned and curious beings who are conscious of their fundamental human rights. They believe in the power of public opinion. The editorial writer should therefore recognize this group of audiences and tailor his/her message to meet their standard and idiosyncrasies.

· **The Very Selective Audience:** These are specialized audiences who care only about what goes on in their chosen fields. They are addicted to the knowledge in their fields or disciplines and are glued to same without bothering about things outside their areas of interest or professional attachment.

For an editorial writer to meet the yearnings and aspirations of this group of people, he/she has to segment his market (editorial) in tandem with the selectivity of this audience.

Experts argue that an editorial can hardly be for everybody at the same time. The editorial writer must mentally define his audience before writing his piece.

The Obscure or Obstinate Audience: These groups of people are blind critics. Anything that is said outside their frame of reference by someone else is wrong. Their worldview is very limited and does not go beyond their local assemblies where they often feed on rumour mongering and worthless *abracadabras* of the day. These groups of people are more of intellectual lumpen and they believe that holding an opinion is a transgression against public order. They are mere chatter-boxes who read editorials not to learn anything but to attack the writers with blind and worthless criticisms.

According to Iyorkyaa (1996:15), this group "does not belong to power. It does belong to the group shaping Beer Parlour Policy (BPP)."

That means that this group of people is irresponsible and uncoordinated members of Homo sapiens who are fond of analyzing public policies from the shallow and at time tipsy In writing an editorial, the writer should out rightly jettison this group of people. This is because, obstinate audience are no audience and cannot appreciate the robust illumination of public policies and

case making stuff which editorials often deal with.

Having a mental picture of your audience as an editorial writer is a right step in a right direction. Any editorialist who writes for "no audience" may end up embarking on a wasted journalistic exercise.

SELF ASSESSMENT EXERCISE

1. Outline the stages in writing a good editorial? 2. Discuss all you know about editorial audience.

THE EDITORIAL PAGE (LAYOUT)

INTRODUCTION

The editorial page of a newspaper carries the corporate elegance of the paper. It is a reservoir of knowledge for readers as diverse audiences often drink from the editorial fountain of knowledge on socio-political and economic issues. The editorial page mirrors the paper because it reflects the corporate logo and identity of the newspaper. It satisfies the yearnings of the audience in the market place of ideas

Importance of the Editorial Page

The editorial page is very important because it gives the paper editorial integrity and credibility. It paves way for corporate journalism and contributes in no small measure to formation of public opinion. But the question now is, what is the editorial page?

The editorial page, according to Ukonu (2005:17), "appears on a special page – the editorial page. The latter carries the newspaper's name, logo or totem and slogan and mission statement." He stresses that whatever is stated on that page belongs to the newspaper as a corporate entity.

No reporter takes credit for editorials in terms of byline. Historically, the editorial was viewed as an article written by the editor. Even today editorials are written by different writers, they still assume to be the creation of the editor.

Different newspapers assign a special page for editorials. However, there are some times when topical issues of public significance compel the editorial to occupy the front page of a paper for the sake of prominence. Ukonu (2005:17) justifies this standpoint and the procedure:

· When an editorial issue is so important that it merits a front-page placement, usual practice is to box it and clearly label it 'Editorial'.

Most editorials – whether front page or editorial page, are boxed, set in bigger body size, wider column width, and separated by black lines (or a pica of white space in ruled publications) instead of white

space or gutters.

Components of Editorial Page

The editorial page is packaged with some aesthetic and attention arresting devices in order to win the affection of readers. Ukonu (2005:19-20) outlines some components of the editorial page. These are:

· Editorial cartoons

· Pictures (photographs). In Nigeria, however, many editorials do not have pictures

· Letters to the editor

· Wider columns, white space (letting in air) can equally be used to direct readers' to the editorial page

· Typographical device can also be used to catch attention. Through the use of different typefaces.

Editorial Cartoons

These are caricatures that are drawn by graphic artists to enliven the editorial page. Editorial cartoons perform the journalistic role of informing, educating and entertaining the readers. Ukonu (2005:29) captures the essence of editorial cartoons: · Cartoons are line drawings used to inform and entertain. Cartoons amuse, yet they are veritable means of exposing social ills. This is why cartoons are referred to as satire in drawing... Cartoons educate, irritate, tickle or tease. They inform, reform and transform.

ETHICS OF EDITORIAL WRITING

In editorial writing, certain things are expected of editors, writers and other media practitioners to adhere to in order to maintain high journalistic standards. They are as follows:

1. **Editorial Independence**: Decisions concerning the content of the news should be the responsibility of professional journalists.

2. Accuracy and Fairness: The public has a right to know that factual, accurate, balanced and fair reporting is the ultimate objective of good journalism and basis of earning public trust and confidence.

A journalist should reframe from publishing inaccurate and misleading information. Where such information has been inadvertently published, prompt correction should be made.

In the course of his duties, a journalist should strive to separate fact from conjecture and comment.

3. Privacy: As a general rule, journalists should respect the privacy of individuals and their families, unless it affects public interest. Information on the private life of an individual or his family should only be published if it infringes on public trust. Publishing of such information about an individual, as mentioned above should be deemed justifiable only if it is directed at: a. Exposing crime or serious misdemeanor.

4. Decency : A journalist should dress and comport him or herself in a manner that conforms to public taste. A journalist should refrain from using offensive, abusive or vulgar language. A journalist should not present lurid details, either in word or picture, of violence, sexual acts, abhorrent or horrid scenes. In cases involving personal grief or shock.

5. Discrimination :A journalist should refrain from making pejorative reference to a person's ethnic group, religion, sex, or to any physical or mental illness or handicap.

6. Reward and Gratification :A journalist should neither solicit nor accept bribe, gratification or patronage to suppress or publish information. To demand payment for the publication of news is inimical to the notion of news as a fair, accurate, unbiased and factual report of an event.

7. Violence: A journalist should not present or report acts of violence, armed robbery, terrorist activities or vulgar display of wealth in a manner that glorifies such acts in the eyes of the public.

8. **Plagiarism** A journalist should not copy wholesale, or in part, other people's work without attribution.

9. **Copyright**: Where a journalist reproduces a work, be it in print, broadcast, art work or design, proper acknowledgement should be accorded by national and international laws conventions.

10. Children and Minors

A journalist should not identify, either by name or picture, or interview children under the age of 16 who are involved in cases concerning sexual offences, crimes and rituals or witchcraft either as victims, witness or defendants.

11. Access to Information

A journalist should strive to employ open and honest means in the gathering of information. Exceptional methods may be employed only if public interest is at stake.

A journalist should, therefore, avoid paying for information, except public interest so dictates.

12. National Interest

A journalist should use his position to enhance national unity, public good and national interest.

13. Social Responsibility

A journalist should promote human rights, democracy, peace and international understanding.

TUTOR-MARKED ASSIGNMENT Enumerate some crucial ethics of editorial writing.